A New True Book

BATS

By Susan Heinrichs Gray

Consultation by Bat Conservation International which is recognized as the international leader in conservation and education initiatives that protect bats and their habitats. Efforts by BCI have resulted in protective legislation for bats worldwide, including saving many of America's most significant bat populations. For more information on how you can help, please contact BCI at the address below.

Bat Conservation International
P.O. Box 162603
Austin, Texas 78716
1-800-538-BATS

CHILDRENS PRESS®
CHICAGO

Many bats have scary faces.

PHOTO CREDITS

© Reinhard Brucker–38

© Bill Ivy–26, 30 (inset)

Root Resources–© Kenneth W. Fink, 11

Tom Stack & Associates–© Roy Toft, 13 (bottom);
© Richard Thom, 45

Tony Stone Images–© James P. Rowan, 34 (left);
© Leonard Lee Rue III, 36; © Norbert Wu, 44

© Merlin D. Tuttle, Bat Conservation International–
Cover, 2, 4, 9, 10, 13 (top), 14, 16 (3 photos), 17
(2 photos), 18, 20 (2 photos), 21, 22, 24, 25 (2 photos),
28, 32 (2 photos), 34 (right), 35, 37, 40, 43

Valan–© Wayne Lankinen, 6

Visuals Unlimited–© John D. Cunningham, 7; © Kjell B.
Sandved, 19 (right); © David L. Pearson, 30

Tom Dunnington, Illustration, 19 (left)

COVER: Lesser long-nosed bat

Project Editor: Fran Dyra
Design: Margrit Fiddle

A17101975698

j
599.4
G79

Library of Congress Cataloging-in-Publication Data

Gray, Susan Heinrichs.
   Bats / by Susan Heinrichs Gray.
      p.   cm.–(A New true book)
   Includes index.
   ISBN 0-516-01064-6
   1. Bats–Juvenile literature. [1. Bats.]
I. Title.
QL737.C5G66   1994
599.4–dc20   94-10468
                                             CIP
                                             AC

TABLE OF CONTENTS

A BAD REPUTATION

Bats have been misunderstood since ancient times. In legends they often appear as evil beings.

In Europe, it was thought that bats lived only in the homes of witches. People in India believed that a bat flying around one's house was an omen of death. Perhaps

Opposite page: Bats resting in a roost

Little brown bats are found throughout most of North America.

bats were so feared
because of their scary
faces. Or maybe it was
because they only come
out at night.

THE REAL STORY

The truth is that almost all bats are harmless. And most bats are even helpful to humans. Many bats eat flies, mosquitoes, termites, beetles, and moths. Some of these insects carry diseases. Others destroy trees and crops. Bats

Harmful insects destroy many trees and crops. Bats help humans prevent this kind of damage when they eat these insects.

help limit the numbers of these harmful insects.

Some bats eat fruit. These bats often carry food to their roost. On the way, they drop seeds and help spread plants to new areas.

Bats live almost everywhere in the world except Antarctica and part of the Arctic. They prefer warmer areas and are found in greater numbers nearer the equator.

All bats can fly. They are active at night and rest

Mexican free-tailed bats are found in the southwestern United States. They like to roost in caves.

during the day. Bats hang upside down when they sleep. Places where bats sleep are called roosts. A roost may have only a few bats, or it may have millions.

9

An insect-eating bat swoops down on a cricket perched on a cactus.

Scientists divide bats
into two main groups—
megabats and microbats.
Megabats are usually
larger than microbats.
They have large eyes
and excellent eyesight.

Some megabats are called flying foxes because their faces look like the face of a fox. They are also called fruit bats because most of them eat only fruit or the nectar and pollen of flowers.

This megabat is called the hammer-headed fruit bat. Megabats live in Asia, Africa, Australia, and the Pacific Islands.

Microbats are usually smaller than megabats. They have big ears and small eyes. Most of them eat insects.

The wingspan of the smallest bats is around 5 inches (13 centimeters). The largest bat measures 6 feet (1.8 meters) from wingtip to wingtip.

There are almost 1,000 species, or different kinds of bats, in these two main groups.

The spectacled
flying fox (above)
and the
little brown bat
in flight (right)

The Gambian epauletted bat is a flying fox bat—as the face shows.

FLYING MAMMALS

In ancient times, people thought bats were birds. But now we know that bats are mammals—the only mammals that fly.

14

The bodies of birds are covered with feathers. The bodies of bats, like those of all mammals, are covered with hair, or fur.

Some bats have very short fur. Bats that roost outdoors often have long, thick fur.

And one bat has almost no fur at all. It is called the hairless bat. Its only covering is a ring of black, bristly hairs around its neck.

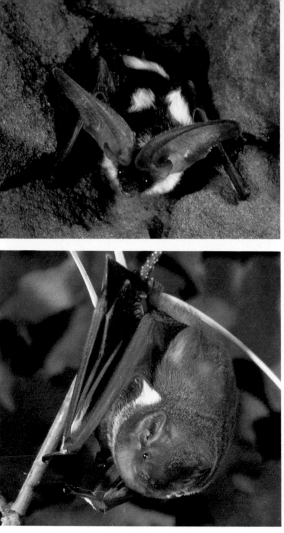

Bats come in many
different colors. Their
fur can be yellow,
orange, white, or even
bright red. Many are
jet black. Ghost bats
are white.

Bats can have brown,
gray, orange, white, yellow,
black, or even red fur.
A few species have white
stripes on their backs

16

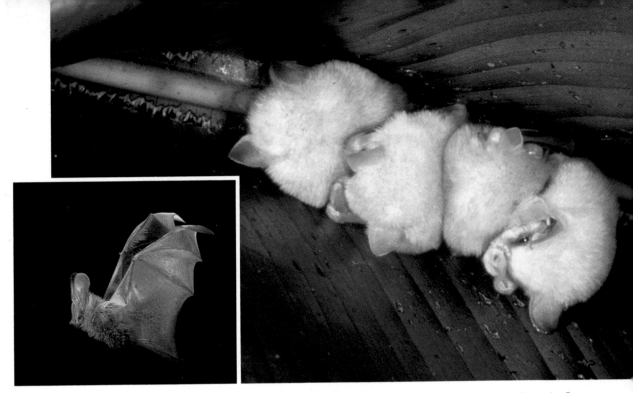

Honduran white bats and a yellow-winged bat (inset). Some microbats have short, stubby wings. They fly slowly but can change directions quickly. Some can hover like a helicopter.

or on their faces. Other species have a single white spot on their shoulders and one on the rump.

The wings of bats are thin, tough, and stretchy. The skin is so thin that

This microbat is called a pallid bat. It has caught a scorpion for a tasty meal.

you can see blood moving through the blood vessels.

The bones of the wings are very much like the bones of a human arm and hand. A bat's "fingers" are very long. Each wing

18

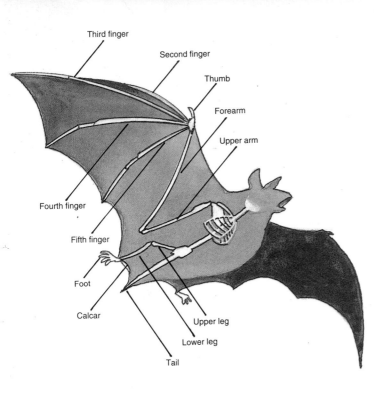

Third finger

Second finger

Thumb

Forearm

Upper arm

Fourth finger

Fifth finger

Foot

Calcar

Upper leg

Lower leg

Tail

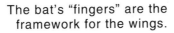
The bat's "fingers" are the framework for the wings.

stretches from finger to finger, down the side of the bat's body, and along the hind leg.

Although bats' wings look hairless, they are covered with many fine hairs.

19

Microbats, like the little brown
bat (left), have small eyes. Megabats,
like the Gambian epauletted
bat (above), have large eyes.

EYES AND EARS

Many people believe
that bats are blind, but all
bats can see. Most insect-
eating bats have tiny eyes
that are hidden in their fur.
Fruit-eating bats have
large eyes that help them
see their way at night.

This flying fox has found a delicious guava fruit.

These bats also have a good sense of smell. This helps them find ripe fruit.

Most fruit-eating bats have short, rounded ears. The ears of insect-eating

21

bats, however, come in many different shapes and sizes. Some are quite large and have a ridged surface. Bats' ears are always twitching, even when the bats seem to be at rest.

Insect-eating bats like this one eat millions of harmful insects every year.

STRANGE NOSES AND KNEES

Some bats have very interesting noses. Several species have nostrils that open at the ends of short tubes.

Bats that suck nectar from flowers have long snouts. These bats stick their snouts deep into

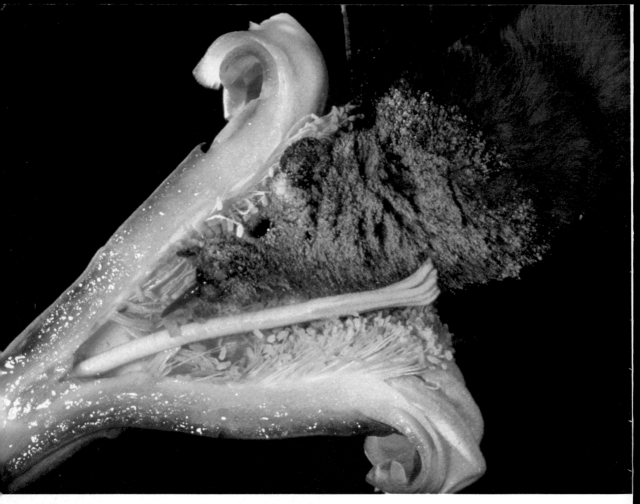

A long-nosed bat feasts on nectar at a cactus flower.

blossoms. Then they shoot
their tongue into the flower
for a tasty meal.

Many bats have folds of
skin surrounding their

nostrils.
Scientists
call this
a nose leaf.
Bats have
rather odd
hind legs
and knees.
In other
mammals,
the knees

Nose leaves surround the
nostrils of some microbats.

The knees of bats are aimed backward, so they cannot walk easily. They prefer to fly.

are aimed forward. But the knees of bats are aimed backward. This makes bats very clumsy when walking or crawling.

Bats have long toes and sharp claws. The claws are strong enough to hold the bat upside down for hours at a time.

"SEEING"
WITH THEIR EARS

Insect-eating bats use sound to "see" their environment. These bats send out sounds from their nose or mouth. Bats often fly with their mouth wide open, making sounds as they travel. The sound waves bounce off objects in the bat's environment.

Some sound waves return quickly. The bat knows these sounds have bounced back from nearby

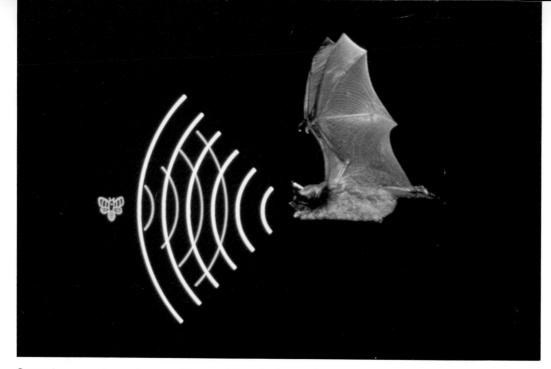

Sound waves have been added to this photograph
to show how echolocation helps bats find insects.

objects. Other sound waves
take longer to return. The
bat knows these sounds
have bounced back from
objects farther away.
Detecting objects in this
way is called echolocation.
  Scientists think that

nose leaves may help in echolocation. Some bats are able to twist their nose leaves around. This may help them aim their sound waves in different directions.

Bats can even tell the direction and speed of a flying insect. By listening to the sound echoes, bats can locate insects in complete darkness. They can also find their way around the roost at night.

LIFE IN THE ROOST

Some fruit-eating bats roost in trees. On cold days they wrap their large wings around their bodies. On hot days they open up their wings and gently fan them. Smaller, insect-eating bats need more shelter. These bats roost in caves, hollow trees, attics, and even in ancient tombs. Carlsbad Caverns, New

Opposite page: Megabats roost together in trees. They wrap their wings around their body (inset) to stay warm.

Bats roosting in Carlsbad Caverns (above). When the bats leave the cave at dusk (inset), it looks as if thick black smoke is pouring from the cave.

Mexico, has a famous roost. Scientists believe that over half a million Mexican free-tailed bats may roost there during the day.

At sunset, the bats

32

begin to leave the cave. Thousands of bats fly out in huge clouds every minute. It looks like thick black smoke is pouring from the cave.

When bats are ready to leave their resting place, they first loosen their grip. As they begin to fall, they flap their wings. Sometimes they almost hit the ground before they fly.

When they return to the roost, the bats slow down their wing flapping. Then

they flip their body around
and grab a good resting
place with their feet.

Some large fruit bats
look clumsy when landing.
They appear to crash into
branches or other bats.

A newborn baby bat
clings tightly to its mother.

A baby Egyptian fruit bat nursing (left) and a
Gambian epauletted bat mother and baby (right)

A megabat mother carries her baby in flight.

The mothers of some
species take babies with
them on flights. Mexican
free-tailed bats leave their
young in their roost, where
they hang upside down
in a group to stay warm.

A returning mother
listens for the call of her

35

A red bat and four youngsters hanging on a wooden beam

own baby. Sometimes the mother and baby call to each other. The mother can then find her own baby among many others.

In some species, the young can fly after about two weeks. Others are not ready until they are three months old.

Vampire bats are the most famous, and the most misunderstood, of all bats.

VAMPIRE BATS

Vampire bats are probably the most famous—and most feared—of all bats. Vampires are found in Mexico, Central America, and in much of South America.

37

The vampire uses its long teeth to cut a shallow wound in its victim's skin.

A vampire's front teeth are large and razor-sharp. The bat uses them to cut a shallow wound in a bird or a large mammal such as a cow or a horse.

The bat then presses its notched lower lip against the wound. It does not suck the blood that flows. It laps the blood up with its tongue.

Vampires are most active on dark, moonless nights. When a vampire spots a victim, it circles the animal several times. Then it

The vampire bat uses its feet and thumbs to hop gently on its victim.

lands, holding its body high and hopping gently along on its thumbs and the soft soles of its feet. In this way, the bat does not alarm its victim.

Vampires are the only bats known to care for young who have lost their parents. And they are the only bats known to help each other feed.

If a vampire cannot find food, it approaches a well-fed bat. The well-fed bat then regurgitates blood for the hungry bat to drink.

A vampire bat that goes hungry for two days will die. So, by helping one another to eat, these bats help the species to survive.

Normally, blood from a wound clots, or hardens. But the saliva of a vampire contains a special chemical that keeps its victim's blood from clotting.

This chemical ensures that the wound from a vampire bat will bleed as long as the bat feeds. Other bats may come and feed at the same wound. A vampire feeds until it is so round and full that it can barely fly.

A vampire bat feeding on a chicken's foot

Scientists are studying
the chemical in the
vampire bat's saliva. It
may be able to break up
blood clots in the blood
vessels of humans.

Scientists study all kinds of bats. They tag them (above)
to follow their movements. And they go into bat caves and
other roosting places to examine them (opposite).

This chemical could help
prevent the heart attacks
sometimes caused by blood
clots. So even the most
feared bat is a valuable
creature. The saliva of the
dreaded vampire bat may
someday save human lives.

WORDS YOU SHOULD KNOW

active (AK • tiv)–moving around

blood vessels (BLUD VESS • ilz)–tubes that carry blood through the body

chemical (KEM • ih • kil)–a substance that acts on other substances to make changes

clot (KLAHT)–blood that has hardened from a liquid to a solid form

echolocation (eh • koh • loh • KAY • shun)–a means of finding objects by sending out sounds and receiving the echoes that bounce back

environment (en • VYE • ron • ment)–the things that surround a plant or an animal; the lands and waters of the earth

equator (ih • KWAY • ter)–an imaginary line around the earth, equally distant from the North and South poles

legend (LEH • jend)–a story from the past

megabats (MEG • uh • bats)–a group of bats that have dog-like faces and large eyes, no true echolocation. Found in Africa, Asia, Pacific Islands, and Australia

microbats (MY • kro • bats)–a group of bats that often eat insects and frequently have strange flaps on or near their nose and different ear and eye shapes.

misunderstood (miss • un • der • STOOD)–not understood; wrongly thought to be or do something

nectar (NEK • ter)–sweet, sugary juices produced by flowers

omen (OH • min)–something believed to predict a future event

regurgitate (rih • GUHR • jih • tait)–to cast up incompletely digested food

reputation (rep • yoo • TAY • shen)–name; stature; standing

saliva (suh • LYE • va)–the liquid produced in the mouth

snout (SNOUT)–a big, flat nose or a long, protruding nose

sound waves (SOUND WAYVZ)—waves in the air that carry sounds

species (SPEE • seez)–a group of related plants or animals that are able to interbreed

termites (TER • mites)–small insects that look somewhat like ants

tomb (TOOM)–a grave; a place where a person is buried

vampire (VAM • pyre)–a bat that drinks the blood of warm-blooded animals

variety (vuh • RYE • ih • tee)–a number of different kinds

victim (VIK • tim)–prey; one who is used or taken advantage of

wingspan (WING • span)–the measurement from the tip of one wing to the tip of the other

INDEX

About the Author

Susan Heinrichs Gray has eighteen years of experience in research, teaching, and scientific writing. She has taught General Biology, Human Anatomy, and Human Physiology at the college level and has been involved in research projects in aquatic ecology, in vertebrate embryology, and in angiosperm development. Ms. Gray has published in a variety of scientific and medical journals and has written numerous papers for pharmaceutical companies involved with new drug development. In addition, she has authored three other New True Books for Childrens Press.

Currently, Ms. Gray is serving as a writer for the University of Arkansas for Medical Sciences. She lives in Cabot, Arkansas, near Little Rock, with her husband, Michael.